LIONS

by Lucy Floyd

Harcourt

Orlando Boston Dallas Chicago San Diego

Visit *The Learning Site!*

www.harcourtschool.com

Lions are very big cats.
People who write about lions
call them the "king of beasts."

The female lion is called a
lioness. The male has a mane
around its cheeks and neck.

Lions are seen in places like this. They do not like to be near lots of trees. Lions need room to move around.

Lions also need to be where they can find meat to eat.

Lions hunt for meat. They seek out other animals. They eat anything they can catch.

Lions have sharp teeth.
They need those sharp teeth
to catch animals. They also
need them to eat the meat.

Back from a hunt, lions greet each other. They rub their cheeks together. Lions seem to like each other!

Lions live together in groups called *prides*. Each pride has a place to live. Other lions are kept out.

Female lions are the real hunters in the pride. They see and hear well. Their speed helps them be good hunters.

Male lions have the job of keeping animals away. Other animals could take meat the pride needs.

Young lions are called cubs.
A cub cannot see at first. The
lioness spends a great deal of
time near her cubs.

This cub needed to be moved. It's too weak to walk so the lioness moves her cub.

Cubs seem to be very
hungry. They feed only on
milk when they are little. In
about six weeks, they should
be eating meat.

Cubs like to play. This
teaches them skills they need.
The lioness teaches them, too.
They will soon know how
to hunt.

The king and queen of
beasts are very big cats.
They also are very beautiful.